The United States

Wisconsin

Paul Joseph
ABDO & Daughters

visit us at
www.abdopub.com

Published by Abdo & Daughters, 4940 Viking Drive, Suite 622, Edina, Minnesota 55435.
Copyright © 1998 by Abdo Consulting Group, Inc., Pentagon Tower, P.O. Box 36036,
Minneapolis, Minnesota 55435 USA. International copyrights reserved in all countries.
No part of this book may be reproduced in any form without written permission from the
publisher.

Printed in the United States.

Photo credits: Archive Photos, Corbis-Bettmann, Peter Arnold, SuperStock

Edited by Lori Kinstad Pupeza
Contributing editor Brooke Henderson
Special thanks to our Checkerboard Kids—Brandon Isakson, Shane Wagner,
Aisha Baker, Grace Hansen

State population statistics taken from the 2000 census, city population statistics taken
from the 1990 census; U.S. Census Bureau.

Library of Congress Cataloging-in-Publiction Data

Joseph, Paul, 1970-
     Wisconsin / Paul Joseph.
     p.   cm. -- (The United States)
     Includes index.
     Summary: Describes the geography, history, people, recreations, and industries
     of the state known as "America's Dairyland."
     ISBN 1-56239-801-6
     1. Wisconsin--Juvenile literature. [1. Wisconsin.] I. title. II. Series: United
States (Series)
     F581.3.J67 1998
     977.75   97-40696
                                           CIP
                                         AC

Revised Edition 2002

Contents

Welcome to Wisconsin

Wisconsin lies in the north-central part of the United States. It is filled with thick forests, rolling hills, and fertile valleys. Within its mitten-shaped outline are nearly 15,000 lakes and rivers. Because of this, Wisconsin is one of America's most popular vacationlands.

The state was named for its main river, which was spelled "Ouisconsin." The name is said to have come from a Chippewa word that means "gathering of waters." It was later changed to the spelling of "Wisconsin."

Wisconsin's nickname is the Badger State. This name came from the Wisconsin **miners**. They dug their homes out of hillsides, just like badgers do. The University of Wisconsin's mascot is a badger.

Wisconsin is also known as "America's Dairyland." Since the first cheese factory was opened in the state in 1864, it has always been one of the leaders in dairy production.

Windpoint lighthouse, Wisconsin.

Fun Facts

WISCONSIN

Capital
Madison (191,262 people)
Area
54,424 square miles
(140,958 sq km)
Population
5,363,675 people
Rank: 18th
Statehood
May 29, 1848
(30th state admitted)
Principal rivers
Mississippi River
Wisconsin River
Highest point
Timms Hill;
1,952 feet (595 m)
Largest City
Milwaukee (628,088 people)
Motto
Forward
Song
"On, Wisconsin"
Famous People
Harry Houdini, Robert La Follette,
Jacques Marquette, Orson Welles,
Thornton Wilder, Frank Lloyd
Wright

*S*tate Flag

*W*ood Violet

*R*obin

*S*ugar Maple

About Wisconsin

The Badger State

Detail area

Wisconsin's
abbreviation

Borders: west (Minnesota, Iowa), north (Michigan,
Lake Superior), east (Lake Michigan), south (Illinois)

Nature's Treasures

The beautiful state of Wisconsin has many treasures in its state. There are thick forests, thousands of lakes, rolling hills, and rich soil for farming.

Almost half the land in Wisconsin is farm land. The state has about 94,000 farms. Nearly half of Wisconsin's farms are dairy farms.

Wisconsin has nearly 2 million cows on its dairy farms! Each year, Wisconsin's cows produce enough milk for 42 million people.

Wisconsin's thick forests are filled with many kinds of trees. People travel from all over the country to see the beautiful colors of the leaves changing on Wisconsin's trees in the fall.

Other treasures of Wisconsin are the Great Lakes of Superior and Michigan. The Mississippi and Wisconsin rivers also run through the state. Grain and other **crops** are carried on big boats called barges.

Along with the Great Lakes and the rivers, the thousands of lakes and streams provide some of the best fishing in the country.

Grain Barges in lock, Mississippi River, Wisconsin.

Beginnings

The first known people to live in Wisconsin were **Native Americans**. Some of them were called the Menominee, Chippewa, Potawatomi, Sauk, and Winnebago.

In 1634, Jean Nicolet of France landed on the shores of Green Bay, Wisconsin. He was the first non-Native American to enter Wisconsin. Nicolet traveled down the Fox River and found a region of wooded wilderness with lakes, rivers, and streams.

French **explorers** began settling in Wisconsin. France took over the region and began building homes, churches, and schools. In 1763, France gave the Wisconsin area to England. And in 1783, England gave the region to the United States.

The United States created the Territory of Wisconsin in 1836. At that time there were around 31,000 people living in Wisconsin. Within about 10 years, the **population** grew to 305,000 people.

People were moving to Wisconsin for wheat farming, lumbering, and dairy farming. Because of the rapid growth of the area, **settlers** of Wisconsin were demanding statehood.

President James K. Polk signed the bill on May 29, 1848, that made Wisconsin the 30th state in the United States.

A Native American camp in the 1800s.

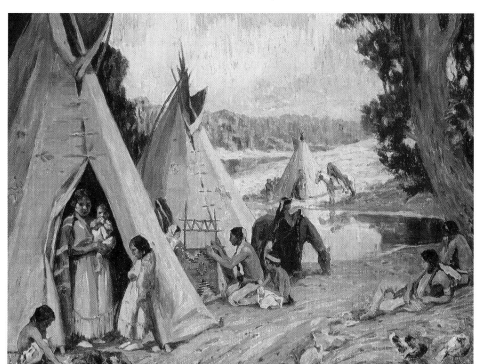

B.C. to 1665

Early Land and Settlers

Many thousands of years ago, Wisconsin was covered by ice and glaciers. Many years later, the ice melted. Wooded wilderness along with lakes, rivers, and streams began to form.

The first known people to live in Wisconsin were **Native Americans**. Some living in Wisconsin were called the Menominee, Chippewa, Potawatomi, Sauk, and Winnebago.

1634: Jean Nicolet of France is the first non-Native American to **explore** Wisconsin.

1665: Father Claude Allouez starts a mission in DePere.

Wisconsin

B.C. to 1665

1763 to 1848

Land Owners to Statehood

 1763: France gives the region of Wisconsin to England.

 1783: England gives Wisconsin to the United States.

 1836: The Wisconsin Territory is formed.

 1848: Wisconsin becomes the 30th state on May 29th.

Wisconsin

1763 to 1848

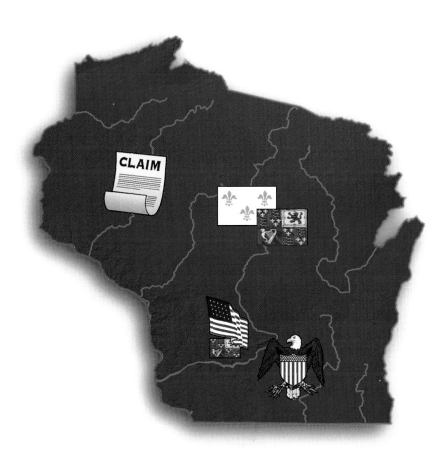

1864 to Today

Present-Day Wisconsin

1864: The first cheese factory in Wisconsin opens in Ladoga.

1961: The bridge over St. Louis Bay between Superior, Wisconsin, and Duluth, Minnesota, is completed.

1993: Floodwaters destroy thousands of acres of farmland and parts of many towns after heavy rains overflow the Mississippi and other rivers.

1997: The National Football League's Green Bay Packers win **Super Bowl** XXXI. The Packers also won the first two Super Bowls in 1967 and 1968.

Wisconsin

1864 to Today

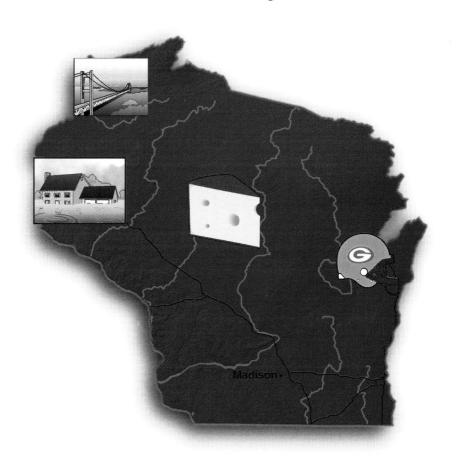

Madison •

Wisconsin's People

There are more than five million people living in the state of Wisconsin. It is the 18th largest state in the country. The first known people to live in Wisconsin were **Native Americans**.

Today, many well-known people have come from Wisconsin. William Rehnquist was born in Milwaukee. After becoming a lawyer, he was chosen to be on the Supreme Court in 1972. In 1986, he was made the chief justice of the highest court in the country.

Speed skater Eric Heiden was born in Madison. At the 1980 Winter Olympics he captured gold medals in all five speed skating events. He also set a world record in the 10,000-meter race.

The legendary actor Spencer Tracy is from Wisconsin. The famous piano player and entertainer Liberace was from Wisconsin, too.

Eric Heiden

Spencer Tracy

William Rehnquist

Splendid Cities

Wisconsin has many splendid cities in its state with many things to do and see. People from Wisconsin live in both large cities and small towns. Many people live out in the country in **rural** areas.

The largest city in the state is Milwaukee. It has over 600,000 people. Milwaukee lies on Lake Michigan in the southeastern part of Wisconsin. It is known for its beer brewing and being the main **manufacturing** center in the state. Marquette University, a well-known college, is in Milwaukee.

Madison is the second largest city in the state and also the capital of Wisconsin. Madison is located in the southern part of the state. Madison is the original home of the

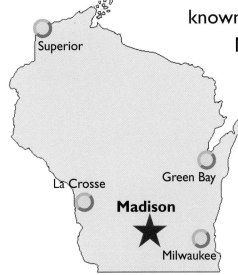

Superior

La Crosse

Green Bay

Madison

Milwaukee

20

University of Wisconsin. Its wonderful lakes and parks make it a very fun place to visit.

Green Bay is a **manufacturing** city. Some of the **industries** in the city include paper products, cheese, and shipping. The city is best known for the Green Bay Packers football team. The team is owned by the city and is one of the most historic teams in all of sports. The "Packer Backers" will sit outside at Lambeau Field even if it is well below zero and the snow is falling, just to watch their home team.

Madison, Wisconsin

Wisconsin's Land

Wisconsin has some of the most beautiful land in the country. Wisconsin is filled with woods, thousands of lakes and streams, many rivers, rolling hills, and fertile valleys.

The land of Wisconsin was formed many thousands of years ago when giant ice glaciers began to melt from the Ice Age. From this melting, Wisconsin's land formed two very different regions. They are the Superior Upland and the Central Lowland.

The Superior Upland region is in the northern half of the state. This area has many lakes and streams. In the very north, Lake Superior meets this region.

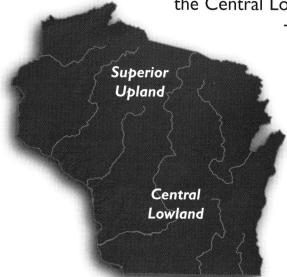

In the south central area of the Superior Upland is Wisconsin's highest point. Timms Hill is 1,952 feet (595 m) tall.

The Central Lowland region is in the southern half of the state. In the middle of this land there are forests, lakes, and streams.

In the western area of the Central Lowland is the Mississippi River. There are many pretty bluffs near this river. On the eastern side is Lake Michigan, which is Wisconsin's lowest point at only 581 feet (177 m).

Wisconsin has beautiful forests.

Wisconsin at Play

The people of Wisconsin and those who visit have a lot of fun things to do in the state all year long. Every part of the state has its own special kind of fun.

Popular vacation spots around the state include Door County in the eastern area. Door County has excellent beaches, great fishing, and other water sports. It is also a great place to cross country ski in the winter.

The Wisconsin Dells, in the south-central part of the state, is a popular **tourist** attraction. The Dells has many water parks, amusement parks, **resorts**, and golf courses.

In the forests in the north people enjoy hunting for bears, partridge, pheasant, ducks, geese, and deer. The many lakes, rivers, and streams throughout the state are great for fishing and other water sports.

In the winter, Wisconsin is still a fun place to play—even with snow on the ground. People enjoy ice fishing, snowmobiling, ice skating, and cross country skiing.

If a person likes to watch sports, Wisconsin offers the best in professional sports. There is the Milwaukee Bucks in basketball, the Milwaukee Brewers in baseball, and the Green Bay Packers in football.

People have fun in Wisconsin.

Wisconsin at Work

The people of Wisconsin must work to make money. There are many different types of jobs in the state. The leading **industry** in the state is **manufacturing**.

The people in Wisconsin that work in manufacturing mostly work in large cities like Milwaukee. Some of the manufacturing industries make engines, farm and garden machines, cheese, butter, milk, or beer.

Many people in Wisconsin work on farms. There are 94,000 farms in the state, and nearly half are dairy farms. Farmers in the state grow many different **crops**. Some are corn, oats, hay, cranberries, and potatoes.

The dairy farmers in Wisconsin help to make dairy products. Dairying is the state's best known industry.

There are many other jobs in the state, too. The people of Wisconsin are teachers, plumbers, police officers, **miners**, and accountants, among others.

Wisconsin offers many things to do and see. Because of its beauty, waters, forests, and people, the Badger State is a great place to visit, live, work, and play.

A dairy farm in Wisconsin.

Fun Facts

•Wisconsin was known for starting many things. Among them was starting the Republican political party, having the first kindergarten class in the United States, and being the first state to use a number system to mark its highways.

•When margarine was first made in Europe in the 1870s as a cheap replacement for butter, dairy farmers in the United States wanted it **banned**. For many years some states didn't allow artificially colored margarine to be sold. Wisconsin was the last state to lift the ban but not until 1967!

•Wisconsin is a leader in cheese making. Its cheese has become famous worldwide. People from Wisconsin are proud of this. They even wear cheese-wedge hats at sporting events.

Cheese production is big business in Wisconsin.

Glossary

Ban: to do away with forever. To not allow something.

Border: neighboring states, countries, or waters.

Crops: the big fields of plants that farmers grow on their land, like corn, beans, or cotton.

Explorers: people that search for new lands.

Industry: many different types of businesses.

Manufacture: to make things by machine in a factory.

Miners: people who work underground to get minerals.

Mission: a place set up so religious leaders can spread their faith to others.

Native Americans: the first people who were born in and occupied North America.

Population: the number of people living in a certain place.

Resort: a place to vacation that has fun things to do.

Rural: outside of the city.

Settlers: people that move to a new land where no one has lived before and build a community.

Super Bowl: the championship of professional football.

Tourists: people who travel for pleasure.

Internet Sites

Wisconsin Summer
http://badger.state.wi.us/agencies/tourism/guide/guide.htm
Spring and summer are the perfect seasons to travel and vacation in Wisconsin. It's a special time in a very special state. Whatever you like, you'll find it here: from big city excitement to Northwood relaxation. Biking, camping, canoeing, fishing, sailing, and horseback riding are just part of the fun. Tour a lighthouse, a cheese factory or a brewery. Sample the charm of a farm vacation. Or, simply enjoy a boat cruise or a train excursion. Discover Wisconsin fun on the land and on the water!

Wisconline
http://www.wisconline.com/
The best way to know what's happening in Wisconsin!

These sites are subject to change. Go to your favorite search engine and type in Wisconsin for more sites.

PASS IT ON

Tell Others Something Special About Your State

To educate readers around the country, pass on interesting tips, places to see, history, and little unknown facts about the state you live in. We want to hear from you!

To get posted on ABDO & Daughters website, E-mail us at "mystate@abdopub.com"

Index